DREAMS, FAIRY TALES, AND MIRACLES

Things I Learned About Success
From Maw-Maw and Paw-Paw Daigle
That You Won't Learn at Harvard or Yale

Believe!
Kerry

KERRY DAIGLE

Designs for Wellness Press
Copyright©2012

First Edition
Copyright © October 2012
By Kerry Daigle

ISBN: 978-1-62154-915-4

Designs for Wellness Press
P.O. Box 1671
Carlsbad, CA 92018-1671
888-796-5229

Senior Editor, Amanda L. Guidry
www.facebook.com/amandalguidrywrites

Assistant Editor, Kate B. Johnson

Cover Artist, Stephanie Martinez
www.smphotodesign.webs.com

Cover photo of Kerry Daigle by Nicole Hood
www.NicoleHood.com

Photo of Dave Bontempo by Donna Connor
www.PhotoFace.com

Public Relations, Andre Courtemanche
www.BigMediaBuzz.com

Printed in the United States of America

For ordering information and volume discounts,
visit our website at: www.DreamsFairyTales.com
or call 888-796-5229 or 760-458-4993.

© Kerry Daigle 2012
www.KeepPunching.com

Here's What People Are Saying About Kerry Daigle's *Dreams, Fairy Tales, and Miracles!*

This is a story of how the front porch of a shotgun home without air-conditioning or hot water was a classroom of meaningful leadership lessons. Kerry shares how he chose the path to success and possibility amid daunting circumstances, for a life so full of pursuing dreams that there is no room for excuses—only priorities. Kerry presents sage wisdom from Maw-Maw and Paw-Paw Daigle in a genuine way that will help readers apply strategic thinking to personal development. This book is full of practical advice that will allow you to also experience dreams, fairy tales, and miracles!

Kathryn Crockett, PhD
Professor of Leadership and Management
Lubbock Christian University

As a former matchmaker for Don King Productions, Inc., I have known and worked with my great friend, Kerry Daigle, for more than 30 years. I have witnessed his guidance of many young boxers to accomplish their goals and enter the rankings of the world ratings bodies. His patience and expertise have enabled these young men to achieve great success. Kerry is also well known and respected in numerous other endeavors, and his work ethic is an inspiration to all who are privileged to know and work with him. His lessons from Maw-Maw and Paw-Paw Daigle will help readers lay out easy steps to achieve success also.

Peyton Sher
Don King Productions

By reading **Dreams, Fairy Tales, and Miracles***, one gets to experience firsthand how Kerry Daigle became what he is. The book, like the man, is inspirational. Kerry's success in the business of boxing and his overall success in life truly teach us to follow our dreams. Knowing Kerry as I do, I really appreciate how sincere his life lessons are, and how beneficial the knowledge he imparts can be if taken seriously and applied. I've known Kerry for many years and deeply respect who he is and what he has accomplished. I am very proud to be his friend. This book is a crowning achievement for a great man and will benefit all who read it.*

Leon R. Margules
Attorney
President of Warriors Boxing and Promotions, Inc.

For as long as I can remember, incredible mentors and teachers have moved in and out of my life, always at just the right time. Twenty years ago, Kerry Daigle showed up—at just the right time. And I have never been the same. His words, his passion, and his insights have already encouraged, challenged, and inspired thousands of people to dig deeper, work smarter, and dream bigger. I'm thrilled that he's finally put those stories, life lessons, and principles for success into this book, **Dreams, Fairy Tales, and Miracles.** *Take the time. Find a quiet spot. Read this book. You will love it!*

David Beavers
Business Coach and Speaker
Author of *Letters to Jonathan*

Kerry Daigle has been a business partner of mine for over 20 years. More importantly, he has been a mentor who has had a tremendous influence and effect on my life. His wisdom and teachings have transformed my life and me as a person. I am a totally different person today than I was when this journey began with Kerry as a mentor. Most of the important things he has taught me came directly from his humble beginnings with his Maw-Maw and Paw-Paw. You too can have your life touched and changed by applying the things you will learn from this book, passed down through the Daigle family. You will be glad you read this book! I sure am.

Dany Martin
Business Owner and Entrepreneur

Kerry Daigle has been instrumental in my personal and professional growth. Kerry has a way of speaking life-changing principles that "pack a punch"! The legacy that was passed down to him, which he is now imparting to the masses, is invaluable. What a gift this book is, to this generation and the next!

Kathrine Lee
Entrepreneur

Kerry Daigle may well be the ultimate poster child for the American Dream—testimony to the unlimited opportunities everyone has in this country. There are tons of rags-to-riches stories of business success in the U.S. This success is so frequently bred from lofty academic degrees and, unfortunately, too often with ruthless traits of character. Not so Kerry Daigle. While the common denominators of personal success are personal responsibility and determination, he, uniquely, has taken these qualities in a much different and softer direction. He was nurtured and educated by grandparents who offered not an academic background but a goldmine of gentle yet practical advice. Kerry's MBA and PhD — "Masterful Blueprint for Accomplishment" and "Personal Habits from the Daigles" — are the "degrees" that guided his success. **Dreams, Fairy Tales, and Miracles** *conveys his personal journey and how he followed that advice from Maw-Maw and Paw-Paw Daigle. And now he shares this goldmine with us. A "must-read"!*

Richard C. Boronow, MD
Clinical Professor of Gynecology, Emeritus
University of Mississippi Medical Center

Kerry Daigle's grandparents believed in him. They believed in his dream, his vision, and his goals for his life. They instilled the attitude that you can accomplish the desires of your heart. Kerry Daigle overcame formidable obstacles on his journey. This book will guide you to become more than a dreamer; you will see the way to become a doer. Get ready to watch your dreams shape your life through intentional action. Live a life of possibility.

Terri Luongo
Certified Fitness Professional

Kerry's life story in **Dreams, Fairy Tales, and Miracles** *is shared in such a way that I could just see myself sitting on that front porch being blessed with the wisdom from his grandparents. This wonderful book has helped me learn some life lessons that I will now share with my children and grandchildren. What a blessing for generations to come to have this as a "life reference book"—I can't wait to share!*

Kathryn McLeod Hess
Entrepreneur

Acknowledgements

I would not have been able to write this book without the support of my wife, Mickey, who encouraged me to finish it for years even though I always had a reason why I didn't or couldn't—isn't it interesting that authors always find a way to put off the writing they so genuinely want to do? Mickey patiently put up with me until I was ready to complete the teachings of Maw-Maw and Paw-Paw Daigle. Putting up with me isn't that easy; I'm always traveling and I stay up into the wee hours so I can think in complete quiet. But Mickey knows the love I carry for my grandparents and wanted me to tell the stories. Thank you, Mickey, for your continued support and love.

Amanda Guidry came into my life as the editor of a newspaper/magazine in Louisiana for which I wrote personal development articles. Thanks, Amanda, for helping to piece these stories together. Thanks also to Gwen Fontenot and Dawna Waterbury for welcoming my stories into their magazines, which led to this book.

My first mentors were Maw-Maw and Paw-Paw Daigle, my grandparents who raised me; they instilled into my life the power of positive thinking, the visions that come from dreams, and the belief that fairy tales do exist in America, all leading to miracles. I am indebted to Clarence Soileau, who taught me how to network as I bartended at his restaurant when I was only 18, meeting the "who's who" of St. Landry Parish in Louisiana, and to R.H. "Buddy" Littell, who financed my first large business. And I appreciate the words of wisdom from Bobby Dupre, who gave me great advice on creating new businesses and believed in my journey to entrepreneurship.

The father-and-son team of William C. "Billy" Sandoz and Sim Sandoz believed in me at times when I didn't believe in myself. Their guidance and encouragement were instrumental, and what I learned from them is invaluable. None of my successes would have happened without their words of wisdom and, most of all, their devotion. It's no wonder they're recognized as top attorneys in their field nationwide. They are in my heart daily, as are Jim Tatman and Charles and Donna Inhern, who stuck with me and encouraged me to continue moving forward during hard times; their belief in me was contagious and kept me focused on the ultimate objectives in life.

I owe a huge debt of gratitude to Peyton Sher, who guided me early in my boxing promotional and management career; assisting him through Don King Productions and Madison Square Garden gave me the experience to become involved in many nationally televised productions. I owe a similar debt to Murray Goodman, a consummate professional, who taught me how to promote through the weekly boxing articles I wrote for a local newspaper. Those great mentors changed my life. Appreciation goes out as well to my attorney friend in Florida, Leon Margules, who gave me tremendous guidance in the boxing industry.

To my boxers, Michael Martinez, Blake Prevost, Skip Scott, and Chad Trahan, thanks for allowing me to watch over you—it is an honor. Thanks to Beau Williford, Deirdre Gogarty, and Bobby Benton for being watchdogs over these wonderful men so I can continue to work and improve my skills, and also to David Rivas for always supporting all my requests, no matter what they were.

My mentors in direct sales are many, and they led to my writing this book. I wish I could list them all, but that's impossible. One person who has stood by me from 1989 through today in building a solid direct-sales business is Elton DuBose; without him, none of this would be happening to me. Elton, I'm very grateful you came into my life and are still always available to consult. I think Elton has a direct line to Maw-Maw and Paw-Paw Daigle.

I want to thank Stephanie Martinez for preparing the book covers, and my daughter-in-law, Nicole Hood, for making me look good on them. Nicole, thanks also for taking care of our son, Cliff, who followed his dream to be in law enforcement. Special thanks for those three wonderful grandchildren, Ali, CJ, and Keri, who can reach into the world and become whatever they want to be. I hope I can be their Paw-Paw Daigle.

My ever faithful, always dependable publisher and consultant, Dr. Roy Vartabedian, is not only a mentor of mine but he also enabled this book to become reality so I can introduce others to my grandparents' wisdom. His guidance as a *New York Times* bestselling author is priceless, and I owe him a particular debt of gratitude. His company's highly capable editor, Kate Johnson, swooped in to help us at the last minute with editing and formatting of the final manuscript and late additions.

Of course, my daughter, Angela, who came into our lives through adoption at the age of six, is my inspiration. To know her story and see her incredible growth over the years continually inspires me to be better at what I do every day. Good luck to you, Angela, as you embark on your dreams at LSU so fairy tales can exist in your life. Miracles will happen for you, as you are a miracle to me.

Finally, I want to thank you, the reader, for wanting to learn from Maw-Maw and Paw-Paw Daigle. I know Maw-Maw and Paw-Paw have been watching me as I prepare this book in their honor. I will honor their request to transfer on to others the gifts given to me by all my mentors.

All those mentioned above as my mentors in life are also my heroes, and I love you.

—*Kerry Daigle*

Contents

About the Author

Kerry Daigle, a proud Cajun from Opelousas, Louisiana, now residing in Lafayette, paints the portrait of the ultimate Renaissance man. A successful entrepreneur since 1965, Kerry runs a number of businesses out of his home while simultaneously hosting a radio show, writing books, and keeping a hectic speaking schedule. The residual income from operating and managing a direct-sales nutraceutical business has allowed Kerry to chase his dreams by giving him the time and freedom so many people lack.

Kerry's businesses take him literally around the world, from Australia to the United Kingdom and throughout the United States and Canada. In speaking engagements with worldwide audiences, he shares insightful presentations full of revealing Cajun wisdom learned from his first mentors, grandparents Maw-Maw and Paw-Paw Daigle. Through the teachings of all his mentors, Kerry would have been able to retire more than comfortably at age 42—if he'd so desired.

Kerry's radio show, *Keep Punching with Kerry Daigle*, offers motivation and inspiration to a global audience that can access archived shows (at www.keeppunching.com) 24 hours a day, seven days a week.

Kerry's tremendous knack for finding and developing talent extends beyond his core business and into his love affair with the sport of boxing. Kerry finds, coaches, and develops promising young fighters, helping them to excel and rise through the professional ranks and into the big leagues. He uses this special gift in all areas of his life, as a mentor and teacher at home, in his businesses, and in other personal pursuits. (Visit www.keeppunching.com, Kerry's sports and sales website, full of information on personal development, sales, book recommendations, and much more.)

Kerry Daigle shows the world, through his actions and accomplishments, that you truly can have it all. You need to believe in your dreams...believe in fairy tales...and miracles do and will happen.

The Daigle Family

Foreword

By Dave Bontempo

I am delighted to write the foreword for Kerry Daigle's hot-off-the-press production, *Dreams, Fairy Tales, and Miracles*. It's partly because, as a regular boxing commentator for HBO, Pay-Per-View, ESPN, and varied regional networks, I've enjoyed his company. And it's partly because I like Kerry's win-win approach, his role of kingmaker, and his quest to unearth the best in human nature. But that's not all.

It's also because this book mirrors qualities anyone would respect: modest roots, tenacity, and dreaming big but retaining perspective. I believe that holding on to one's friendly qualities, as Kerry has, is important. Congeniality in a dog-eat-dog world is a badge of class.

Having his own high-profile company, I suspect Kerry derives satisfaction from achieving affluence despite growing up with no running water, no air-conditioning, and secondhand clothes. Casino presidents have told me similar anecdotes about walking around with holes in their shoes and standing in line for food as youngsters. Their humility shines through their ascent to multimillionaire status. Having faced sink-or-swim mandates at early ages, they swam.

Kerry reminds me of their perspective and indomitable spirit. I believe that Maw-Maw and

17

Paw-Paw Daigle, among his other mentors, taught him to find an alternative to "no." Kerry speaks of surrounding yourself with winners, working for something you'll own, and compiling nuggets of information from successful people.

Is that in itself new? No. What is novel is that these truths, though contained in a book, did not come from one. They originated from real people whose impacts multiplied through their stature in his life. Those people supplied pieces of a puzzle, unaware of how he would put them together.

Kerry demonstrates that how a person connects strands of information and inspiration will often determine how far he rises. His mantra of being a student and having a mentor propelled him to business ventures he might otherwise have considered unreachable.

Once success is achieved, the process can be honored by passing the lessons along, and Kerry has done that too. He'll provide someone with half of the treasure map if that person will work to achieve the other half. In all cases, Kerry presents opportunity.

When I view his achievements, his success is not measured by how many books he's published, how well his nutraceutical products have per-formed, or the fact that for the past decade he hasn't been forced to work. Kerry's success, to me, stems from who he is.

My first regular contact with him came in the natural relationship between fight managers and media people. We expect managers and promoters to speak kindly, put their best foot forward, and bring out every positive element of their fighter, whether the topic is a special new regimen, a change to the team, or a distraction that may have affected a recent fight. Much of this discussion is designed to portray the fighter in the most marketable terms possible. Commentators who translate a positive item gleaned from pre-fight production meetings into the telecast lift fighters immeasurably.

It was not surprising, therefore, that Kerry was unfailingly kind, smiling, upbeat, and well-versed on the big picture connecting networks and fighters when we first worked together. He was, as I saw it then, doing his job. As time went on, however, a subtle reality emerged: Kerry was always this way.

Darned if I could find a more unflappable, optimistic personality, with natural deal-making instincts. Kerry describes himself as a kingmaker, someone willing to help other people realize dreams. First, he helps people see them.

When Kingfish Boxing unfurled a series a decade ago, Kerry approached me one evening in Lafayette, Louisiana. He told me I should be writing about my commentating journey—from ESPN to Pay-Per-View and HBO, from countless road trips, from five-dollar to five-star hotels. This now 28-year run includes calling fights on the world's highest stage, he said. The ledger includes Tyson-Lewis, Bowe-Holyfield, and most fights involving Oscar De La Hoya, Floyd Mayweather, and Roy Jones Jr. Throw in the documentaries, the Gatti-Ward trilogy, distinctions like the Boxing Writers Association of America's Sam Taub Award, and your induction into the New Jersey Boxing Hall of Fame, he said.

Kerry noted I'd partnered with every conceivable high-level broadcaster, from Al Bernstein and Bob Papa to Gus Johnson and Teddy Atlas. "You've got that light surrounding you which gives off so much good energy," he told me. "People see it and they want it."

Kerry suggested developing a public speaking program wrapped around the book I should write. It was a startling piece of insight from someone not in the media business. And he convinced me…but circumstances intervened.

Long story short, I launched six chapters, and then the boxing series, which would have been the book's distribution arm, abruptly stopped. One month later, my Mother suffered a heart attack, and I spent the next two years helping her meet a dignified passing. The book fell to the side, while my broadcast and writing gigs remained strong, and Mother's passing inspired a community-minded route: for seven years, I've contacted elderly people every Monday in their homes for United Way's Contact Cape-Atlantic, a ritual that's produced deep-seated bonds of friendship. Now I write two stories a month for their newsletter too.

These things help me live with my "unfinished literary symphony." But I never forgot that Kerry was right to suggest I do a book. His wisdom resurfaces whenever other commentators publish the type of product I'd like to have finished, about living the dream. My buddy Al Bernstein just finished his and equated the experience with giving birth. (Maybe it was a Caesarian.)

I would have called my book *You Don't Need a Rich Uncle*, referring to succeeding in life without contacts. Though autobiographical, the message was bound to make people feel even better about themselves. There's a way to enlist the help of secretaries, production assistants, and top executives to prevent important doors from slamming in your face. I know it, I've done it, and I still do. (I can extend this message to any organization in a public-speaking format; simply contact me at daveybontheair@comcast.)

In the meantime, enjoy Kerry's book. He has an excellent grip on human nature, an empathy one can't manufacture, and a solid list of intangibles. Gravitate toward his type of energy and think win-win.

Then you can experience some fairy tales too.

Donna Connor (PhotoFace.com)

Dave Bontempo

One of the most versatile announcers in the television industry, Dave Bontempo has called some of the biggest fights in boxing history, either as a blow-by-blow commentator or color analyst. Since 1984, the New Jersey native has broadcast in prime time on every major network including HBO, Fox, Showtime, ESPN, and Comcast, as well as several regional networks.

Known for his enthusiasm and even-handed portrayal of competing fighters, Dave has been honored by the Boxing Writers Association of America for excellence in broadcasting and gained induction into the New Jersey Boxing Hall of Fame.

Some of Dave's biggest calls included the 2002 Tyson-Lewis fight, broadcast to approximately 130 countries. He has covered many bouts involving Evander Holyfield, Roy Jones Jr., Arturo Gatti, Floyd Mayweather, and Oscar De La Hoya.

Before entering broadcasting, Dave won several awards issued by the New Jersey Press Association for his boxing coverage featured in the press of Atlantic City.

Dave managed his accomplishments with virtually no connections. He now uses his experience to motivate both individuals and businesses. (To schedule a speaking engagement for his presentation, "You Don't Need a Rich Uncle," contact Dave at daveybontheair@comcast.net.)

A Note from the Editor

By Amanda L. Guidry

My part in this book is small compared to Kerry's, as he is drawing from his own personal conversations with his grandparents. But I chose to be part of this endeavor because I agree with his and Maw-Maw and Paw-Paw Daigle's attitudes toward life and living.

When I first read Kerry's proposed title, my eyes nearly popped from their sockets, for it embodied two truths that I wholly support: 1) education and intelligence are two different things, and 2) fairytales and miracles do happen.

I suppose Kerry's collection of his grandparents' wise teachings is common sense, but the fact is that people rarely stop and think out these concepts. In today's fast-paced and cut-throat society, we often forget to slow down, smell the proverbial roses, and dwell on the important things in life.

So take a few minutes from your hectic schedule and read a chapter or two each day. And keep in mind, if you put your mind to it, you can accomplish anything.

About the Editor

Most children scribble and draw when their parents hand them paper and pencil to keep them quiet during church, but Amanda L. Guidry opted to write stories, completing her first tale at the ripe old age of four. That story, "The Miller's Daughter," lives in the annals of her mother's memorabilia collection in southwest Louisiana, the beloved Cajun country Amanda calls home.

From the first time she placed pen to paper, she knew she was destined to write stories. She earned bachelor's and master's degrees in communication and journalism from the University of Louisiana at Lafayette so she could "earn a practical living" in writing while pursuing her dream of being a novelist. After working as the managing editor of a newspaper and teaching part-time at her alma mater and Louisiana State University at Eunice, Amanda made a switch; she now pursues freelance writing and editing ventures while also teaching creative writing, English, and public speaking at a high school that focuses on the cultural arts.

E-mail: amandalguidry@yahoo.com
Facebook:
www.facebook.com/amandalguidrywrites

A Note from the Author

Every workshop I've been to, every motivational speaker I've heard in person or on a
CD…everything they've said has been something Maw-Maw and Paw-Paw Daigle told
me—in just a slightly different way.

So I started telling people about things
Maw-Maw and Paw-Paw said, and people
wanted to hear more about them, which is why
I chose to compile some of their teachings in
this book.

People have forgotten how to dream; they
need to know that life is full of fairy tales and
that miracles do happen. If you dream enough,
and if you believe in fairy tales, truly believe,
then miracles happen. I didn't have a formal
education. I'm a high school graduate. I just
followed a dream. If you dream big, your
world's big. If you dream small, your world
will be small.

There is a quote one of my mentors left
with me: "If you shoot for the moon and miss,
you will still be among the stars." There is so
much truth there. When I was young, Paw-
Paw always made me look at the moon late at
night, believing that if you took some quiet

time at night, relaxing, looking at the moon…dreams would appear. Good dreams.

Thanks, Paw-Paw. They have.

The only way to find happiness is to look within your heart and start dreaming; the only way to experience fairy tales is through the imagination and power of the mind and heart; the only place to begin a search for miracles is within your soul; because dreams, fairy tales, and miracles are treasures that grow from the inside of your soul and within your heart. Always believe in your dreams...become a kid once again and believe in fairy tales, and miracles will happen.

KEEP PUNCHING!

Kerry Daigle

www.dreamsfairytales.com
www.keeppunching.com
www.kerrydaigle.com
www.kmdteam.com

Introduction

Everyone goes through hard times in one way or another. Sometimes that's an advantage.

I was born in a Charity Hospital in Lafayette, Louisiana, and raised by my grandparents, Maw-Maw and Paw-Paw Daigle. They were both illiterate and spoke only French—not a word of English—and they were my first mentors. You'll come to know them as you read this book. (In these pages, you don't hear about my birth mother, Viola Miller: In 1996, when I was in my forties, we had the opportunity to be reunited after my wife, Mickey, and a friend, Donna Inhern, made it their mission to find her. Today, she's in her eighties and doing exceptionally well, and we communicate regularly.)

I grew up understanding the value of a dollar. I had a paper route at the age of nine and started my own lawn service at 11. At 13, I opened my first home-based business in my grandparent's shotgun house—to this day, I still operate all of my businesses out of my home. For extra income at 15, I worked on a milk truck for $1.50 a day plus all the milk I could drink.

After graduating high school, I started promoting amateur boxing at 18 while bartending at night. By the time I was 21, I was promoting professional boxing, and in my early twenties I was earning a six-figure income. The power of my mentors prepared me for the life lessons that were to come. That was the rule, and that was my education: no BA, MA, or PhD degrees, just LE—Life Experiences.

Things were bright until I had to declare bankruptcy at age 31. By then my grandparents were deceased, so I couldn't go home to them. For a time, sleeping in my car and hiding out from everyone became the norm. That was a hard period, when everything was being repossessed, including my home. It seemed as though the harder I worked, the larger the hole I fell in.

In times like that, you have to look deep into yourself and remember that people can take away your finances but they can never take away your skills. If I had accepted defeat, I wouldn't be passing this book on to you now. I had to remember all the teachings from all my mentors and realize what could be done versus what could not be done. I kept hearing Maw-Maw and Paw-Paw talking to me about being grateful for what God did offer me in the value of my mentors and the skills I'd developed over the years, and to use them again and again. After all, I knew what poverty was. I was born into it. I was prepared to battle it again and take life on because I had no other choice.

The lessons in this book may seem simple, but as you read its chapters about the wisdom of Maw-Maw and Paw-Paw, you'll be reminded that failure is a temporary condition, just a learning curve to test your intestinal fortitude to succeed, and that life is nothing more than a report card to see what kind of grade you'll make. I was born into state assistance and then enjoyed the life of a king, only to end up on the charity of friends and mentors. Coming back from a knockdown is not an easy thing, but getting up from a knockdown is what's necessary to move forward and be a winner in life.

Understand there will always be good times, hard times, and other times that will test your sanity. In those times, you must be aware of who you are and what you want to become. Reading the right books to help yourself grow personally and find mentors is crucial to your success. I hope this one will inspire you enough to share with other friends, peers, and family. (That's why I've arranged with the publishers to offer the books in quantity at incredible discounts.)

The naysayers will always be there. Where do they come from? Who knows...but they sure know when to show up, don't they? Relieve yourself of them as soon as you can, or at least from the conversation of negativity.

Dreams are the lifeblood of your success. Mark Twain wrote, "Don't give up on your dreams. When they are gone you may still exist, but you've ceased to live." Maw-Maw believed in the power of the dream and would purposely encourage me to dream every night; so I believed my destiny was going to happen, fairy tales would exist, and if you continued with that attitude, miracles would happen. Of course, none of this is true without some sweat equity and work to go with it.

Today, I work for you and your testimony. My finances are good, and because of the wonderful people I've met along this journey called life, it's time for me to pay back through the power of mentorship. All I work for now is the testimony. I hope I can one day get a testimony from you after gifting you with the lessons from Maw-Maw and Paw-Paw Daigle and many of my later mentors.

Keep punching!

The Front Porch

By Amanda L. Guidry

The modest house at 1257 South Railroad Avenue in Opelousas, Louisiana, wasn't fancy. It was wooden. It wasn't even a brightly painted white clapboard house—just plain, old wood, weathered to a dull grayish-brown. It had a wooden porch, four wooden posts, and steps framed by a handrail. The entrance consisted of a squeaky screen door and an old wooden door, and one window overlooked the street on the right end of the porch.

For most houses, the front porch is simply the steppingstone to the actual home, the dwelling center for the family that holds sleeping children and chatting parents. But for Kerry Daigle, the front porch *was* home. It was where his grandparents, Maw-Maw and Paw-

Paw Daigle, taught him life lessons, pulling from their experiences to pass down their homespun wisdom.

It was the family meeting place for after-dinner talks. It was the gathering place for friends. It was the confessional. It was the mecca of the Daigle family.

And if passersby strolled or drove along Railroad Avenue, Maw-Maw and Paw-Paw Daigle would send out friendly waves and smiles, usually getting a few friendly gestures in return.

Young Kerry would sit beside his grandparents—they on handmade wooden chairs with cowhide seats, and he sitting near them on the floor—embarrassed. "Why," he asked, "do you wave to everybody like that?"

His grandparents, smiling the smiles of wisdom borne of experience, replied simply, "They don't know us, but we can show them how to be friendly."

Today, decades later, Kerry remembers the incident with fondness, smiling his own smile of wisdom. That was one of his first life lessons, he says.

"Maw-Maw and Paw-Paw were helping these people to understand they needed to slow down and be nice," he explains. Kerry leans back in his office chair, envisioning his grandparents with love and respect, before continuing, "These older people are the wise people, and the wise people, you can learn from. And if you listen, listen carefully, then you can learn life lessons."

Paw-Paw and Maw-Maw Daigle

Find a Mentor

As we sat on the porch on South Railroad Avenue in Opelousas, my grandparents, Maw-Maw and Paw-Paw, waved at everyone who passed by, a ritual that evolved over the years. I remember sitting with them, watching the traffic flow. I leaned over and asked Paw-Paw how those people could afford those nice cars. What did they do?

Here is what Paw-Paw told me: "Son, never think someone else can do better than you. Believe in yourself and good things will happen. If you hang around a shoplifter, you will learn how to shoplift. If you hang around successful people, you will learn how to be successful. And remember, 'dream big.' If you dream big, your world is big; if you dream small, your world is small."

*   *   *

Most of us have heard the word *mentor* and formed a belief about what it means. Webster's dictionary defines it as "a wise, trusted teacher or guide." Although we may understand the literal meaning, few of us fully grasp the true value of mentors.

I opened up my first home-based business in Maw-Maw and Paw-Paw's home back in 1965, at the age of 13. I decided to sell used toys to the other kids in the neighborhood.

Before getting started, I knew I needed to get advice from one of my most trusted mentors, Paw-Paw Daigle. Uneducated in the sense that he could neither read nor write, Paw-Paw possessed great wisdom, which he dispensed only in French, his native tongue.

I asked Paw-Paw how some people became so successful while others didn't. It didn't seem fair.

I attended Opelousas Junior High School, and most of the kids had parents who brought them to school in nice cars. They wore nice clothes. I had to walk to school since we didn't own an automobile, and I wore secondhand clothing given to me by the neighbors.

My friends had something called air-conditioning in their home. We didn't. They had hot water running through their faucets. We didn't.

They had someone to sit with and teach them reading and writing. Maw-Maw and Paw-Paw couldn't do either, and they spoke only French. Even though my Dad lived with us, he had such severe glaucoma that he was legally blind. At one time he could read, but now he couldn't see.

I had a hard time understanding the huge disparity between us and the other families.

But Paw-Paw answered my question about success with these simple but truthful words:

Hang around positive people and positive things will happen to you. Hang around negative people, and negative things will happen to you. You choose which direction you need to go in life. You always make the final decision. Find successful people to learn from and watch everything they do. That, my son, will be your education!

What he said made sense. Although I didn't know it then, Paw-Paw had introduced me to the power of mentorship.

*   *   *

When I was growing up, if a boy wanted to become an excellent lawn man and master the art of mowing lawns, he had to hang around people like Mr. Chevis, an expert in lawn cutting. Mr. Chevis took me under his wing and taught me the ropes. Before long, I had my first lawn job, and it grew from there.

I remember all of my customers well: The Mullers on Parkview Drive; Mrs. Muller's mother, Mrs. Dejean, and her husband (the marshal—what a connection that turned out to be); the Mornhinvegs, with their cars and air-conditioners; and the Fontenots, wealthy people with hot water and something called a refrigerator and a black-and-white television set.

I wanted some of those finer things, too.

Mr. Chevis taught me so much. He acted as a source of guidance, advice, and inspiration. As a lawn man, he was the best. He taught me the basics and I listened. I felt lucky to learn at such a young age. He even taught me how to get referrals—funny how we do that today in every phase of business. Today, people pay me good money to teach them how to get referrals for their businesses.

Thank you, Mr. Chevis. I know you're out there listening somewhere.

*   *   *

Paw-Paw's wisdom brought me the vision I needed to find mentors, which I have since done throughout my life.

He and Maw-Maw gave me the spirit to succeed, the passion you can't learn in school, the intestinal fortitude to move forward regardless of your financial and educational situations, and a different type of vision—a vision to believe in yourself and see what others cannot see.

I've never seen or heard of anyone moving backward in life as a result of having a good mentor. It simply astonishes me to hear, as I ask around, that so few people seek them out. Perhaps they feel they know it all and should be, if anything, the teacher.

I've seen many teachers fail in life because they quit being students.

Don't get me wrong. I believe in teaching others what you know, but keep in mind: it's what you don't know that counts.

Always *be* a student.

Always *have* a mentor.

I have several mentors in my life today, some of whom I've never met except in books or videos, or on tapes, CDs, or DVDs. Others I talk to every day on the phone or in person.

Some mentors assist with my business, others in the marketing of my books, promotions, public speaking, networking, and as an agent of professional prizefighters.

The advantages of being a student speak for themselves.

If you sit with successful people in specific fields, become their friend, and adopt them as mentors, you gain confidence, ideas, goals, and road-maps to success.

The mentors also win. They feel good about helping and being acknowledged, about giving back.

Remember that people don't care how much you know; they want to know how much you care. Sometimes it's not about how much the mentors know, but how much they care about giving back.

And it shows. They don't have to tell anyone of their good deeds. Others speak for them.

A mentor does not have to be a person in the flesh. It can be a book, video, DVD, or an audio series, as I mentioned earlier. If it's an individual, it can be someone you speak to once a month or every other month.

When you find that mentor, make it clear that you don't know everything and that you want to learn!

I remember days when I would spend the last dollar in my wallet to buy someone lunch so I could learn from him. What an education!

*   *   *

One of my mentors, Ken Pontius, passed away recently. Ken sat on the board of directors of a direct sales organization with me. He will always be my mentor, and I can still hear his wise words: "Kerry, five frogs sit on a lily pad and three decide to jump off. How many are left?"

Seemed pretty simple, even to a Cajun boy like me. "Two," I'd answer.

Ken would grin as only he could. He'd squint those penetrating eyes and say, "No, Kerry, it's five! Just *deciding* to do something isn't the same as *doing* it. They decided to jump off, but they didn't. Jumping is the key. It's the only thing that matters."

Ken made things happen.

He moved forward and jumped.

You could never pay for a meal with Ken. No matter how hard you tried or how many sat in attendance at the table, he took care of the bill.

In business, he made the first move when others were still thinking about whether something needed to be done.

He made me think I was special, and I watched how he did that with everyone.

He was so humble, and he spread his knowledge to the friends who worked with him.

It didn't matter that Ken made more money in a month than the president of the United States made in a year. He showed all of us that dreams could be reached.

Ken, Paw-Paw and Maw-Maw, and Mr. Chevis are watching me now, and I hear them, every day.

I often asked all my mentors how I could repay them for their guidance and wisdom. Their answers always mirrored each other: "The best way to repay your mentors is to promise them that once you reach a position of success in your life, you pass on the gift of mentoring. Do the same for someone else."

To move to the next level in your business, profession, or any aspect of your life, find a mentor and surround yourself with winners.

Maw-Maw and Paw-Paw said so. And they've been right so far.

Maw-Maw and Kerry

Maw-Maw's Gifts

By Amanda L. Guidry

The old house on Railroad Avenue was home. Trains thundered on the nearby tracks, their noise, energy, and rhythmic vibrations lulling Kerry to sleep after a long day of marble-playing and climbing the oak tree in the backyard. The boy slept the sleep of the exhausted, while the silence left in the train's wake was poignant and as thick as Louisiana's humidity.

When Kerry woke in the morning, he would hurry through breakfast and rush to his friends' homes where he joined the other boys in hardy games of football. And later, through the side kitchen window, Maw-Maw Daigle would call out at the top of her lungs, "Kerry! Kerry!" It was time for lunch, and Kerry would abandon his friends and race home to enjoy his grandmother's cooking.

Meals in the Daigle house were savory and succulent, despite the family's tight budget. "The big meal for us was Thanksgiving," recalls Kerry, closing his eyes and conjuring up images from long ago. "The Thanksgiving meal was a whole chicken. Maw-Maw made home-cooked meals. I don't know how she took the little food we had and spread it out among everybody—just like money for the bills, I don't know how she did that either."

But making both ends meet was Maw-Maw's specialty, her gift, so to speak. She claimed everyone has a gift and she taught Kerry this philosophy.

"Everybody's got a gift," he says. "Don't think of what you can't do, but what you can. That helps you develop it. People spend too much time on how to take care of people's deficiencies when my grandparents did the opposite—my grandparents focused on my gifts."

Listen...and Open Up Your World

I never thought Maw-Maw Daigle would teach me how to sell. Later in life, I realized she taught me more than any seminar, book, or audio program ever did. She taught me that if I listened and asked the right questions, I could resolve any conflict and help people solve their problems. Without knowing it at the time, she also taught me that I could close any sale using the same technique.

On our porch I learned the most valuable lessons for my success. Maw-Maw always said, "God gave you *two* ears and *one* mouth for a reason." And Paw-Paw added, "Sometimes first impressions can fool you. You never know who or what they know or where they can lead you."

*   *   *

At times we may need to listen to what we believe are poor opinions. We may want to say, "That is the dumbest thing I have ever heard. Why don't you get on out of here?"

In those moments, we need to train ourselves to listen and respond, not to react. If we pause, pay attention, and listen, we gain something from another person. If we don't, we never will. We may as well write him off.

Paw-Paw often told me, "Never pre-judge anyone, at anytime. Listen and ask the right questions so you can learn more about them and their background. They may be the person to bring you to the next level in your life or career. Always *listen*, don't just hear what they have to say."

We should never pretend to know what we don't, nor should we feel ashamed to ask and learn from people in all walks of life—blue-collar, white-collar, and everything between. We must keenly hone our listening skills.

Everyone you meet loves to be heard and to speak about themselves and their background. If you start a conversation with the *right* questions, people will give you all the information you want.

Is it hard to develop listening skills? You bet! Recent research showed that working parents listen to their children an average of 1 hour a week, and husbands and wives spend less than 1 hour a week in meaningful conversation with each other.

We have serious work cut out for us.

*   *   *

Earlier, I mentioned that people don't care how much you know; they want to know how much you care. This simple statement implies that people don't want to listen to you talk about everything you know, but would rather be heard, acknowledged, and noticed.

Listening shows we care. Telling someone we care about them isn't as effective as listening to their needs, goals, dreams, desires, and thoughts.

When we talk to them, regardless of our intentions, it's about us. When we listen, it's about them and it shows how much we care.

When people you speak with know you care about them and their goals, they will strive to give you what you need. As Zig Ziglar, the well-known motivational speaker, often said, "Give enough people what they want, and you will receive much more in return."

If you listen to someone else's life goals, opportunities will open up for you.

Ask yourself this question: "Do you really listen to what others have to say, or do you simply wait for your turn to speak?"

Try this experiment. Say something nice to someone today, then ask that person about him- or herself. Be curious, not threatening. Do it with a smile.

If you do this on a regular basis, shift from talking to listening, a whole new world will open up for you. Your personal relationships will grow, as will your business.

*   *   *

Whenever Maw-Maw would remind me about listening being an incredible skill, I'd immediately remember what she said about God giving us *two* ears and *one* mouth. Most of the time, unfortunately, the reverse appears true.

Recently, I spent some time with a salesperson I'll call Bob, who told me about an interview with a promising prospect I'll call Jim. Bob had attempted to bring Jim into his direct-sales business as a partner by talking about the benefits of running his own business in the convenience of home so he could be with his kids on a regular basis.

Jim had incredible potential as a business partner but offered resistance to what Bob was saying. Bob reacted immediately to each of Jim's comments, and Jim kept resisting.

Finally, Jim shouted out to Bob, "I could never work with you! My kids are all grown up, in their mid-twenties, don't work or go to school, and don't want to work or go to school and constantly ask me for money. I want an opportunity to travel, start a new life, meet new and more people, and grow personally. My wife has been deceased for seven years now, and I need to be around different people."

By not asking questions, Bob had made a crucial mistake. He'd talked too much and chosen not to listen to Jim's needs, and he lost a great prospect. Instead of getting into a conversation with Jim, Bob had launched into a presentation. No questions. No discussion. Too much talking and not enough listening.

That scenario happens every day.

Think about it. Would you rather purchase from someone who's constantly selling and talking, or from someone with the decency to respect and listen to your needs, concerns, and desires?

Again, people don't care how much you know; they want to know how much you care.

Talking too much has a tendency to *push* a person into an uncomfortable place. Think about the familiar term "pushy salesmen." They push you away.

When we listen, we *pull* someone toward us, like a magnet.

Talking too much to someone is like trying to push a rope. It simply will not work. But pull the rope slowly, and success will follow.

Ask questions, then listen. Listening leads to better relationships with our children, our spouses, our business partners, and other prospects.

*　　　　　*　　　　　*

Let's look at another example of how to become an effective listener.

Assume someone calls, unhappy, and talks to you in an angry tone of voice. If you answer back with the same angry tone, you may win the argument, but in the long run, you will lose the fight.

You'll create animosity. People will tell everybody about your terrible disposition. You can't win.

Now, consider a different approach: Acknowledge that the person is angry and unhappy. Respect his present feelings. Answer compassionately, and ask him calmly about his problem. "It sounds like you're upset about this situation. Why do you feel this way?"

Ask calm questions. Respond instead of merely reacting. Listen.

You'll be delightfully surprised by the results. That's a promise.

Paw-Paw was a master at listening and asking questions. Before I knew it, he would have me talking myself into doing what he needed or wanted done. I keep thinking of his patient style but alarming ease in "closing the deal"…whatever it was.

Paw-Paw Daigle

Gratitude and Joi de Vivre (Joy of Living)

By Amanda L. Guidry

Sitting on that old wooden porch, Kerry sometimes complained. After all, they had none of the usual amenities, no hot water, just an old gas heater—unlike Stanley Muller's parents, four houses down, who often invited Kerry over for dinner and seemed to be the wealthiest people in the world. And what about Larry Joubert's parents? Larry's father was in the automobile business, so they had money and could afford everything their children wanted.

Meanwhile, the Daigles lived on state assistance. Kerry's father, who lived with them, received a small check for Assistance for the

Blind, and his grandparents received old-age pensions, which totaled $310 a month.

But when Kerry began to complain, his grandparents began teaching him.

"We sat out on the porch during every rain," says Kerry. "I was taught to appreciate everything. Not, 'Oh, the weather's bad.' We'd sit on the porch and see how beautiful the rain was."

"Gratitude is important. Don't complain because it's a thunderstorm, but see the beauty of it," he continues, his voice rising with his words. "My grandmother would say thunderstorms come because God's angry at something and he wants you to pay attention."

And Kerry did pay attention. He soon learned to help out instead of complaining about lack of funds. He mowed lawns, helped his grandmother with the laundry she took in from neighbors (for which she charged 5 cents apiece, and eventually started his own secondhand toy store from a spare room.

He paid attention and decided to make his own luck, to create his own fortune.

Let Friends Happen

Feeling less fortunate than most in our neighborhood, I suffered from an inferiority complex. We seemed so far behind everyone else financially.

I always tried very hard to make friends, but those feelings made it a difficult task for me. My efforts seldom worked. I tried too hard.

One day, after I'd gotten quite upset with my failure, Paw-Paw called me to the porch. "Don't worry about making friends," he said. "Keep good company and seek out quality people. Friends will happen."

I know some of you may wonder what he meant by not making friends; it may sound cold! However, I'd like to explain his philosophy.

63

Paw-Paw was put on this earth to live into his eighties and transfer his life's experiences to those smart enough to listen. He didn't have a BA, BS, or PhD after his name. He had what I call an LE, for Life Experiences, and he could deliver his message better than any person alive.

He taught us to pay the price for success. He reminded us that problems were only obstacles that created opportunities to test us, to see what we were really made of.

And he always said, "If you keep good company, good company will lead you to quality people."

Paw-Paw taught me to surround myself with people who enrich and empower me, people who enable me to transcend limitations and grow personally in a positive direction.

These people—because of their attitudes in life—bring strength in times of weakness, lifting the spirit up instead of pushing it down.

*   *   *

Most of us can acknowledge that we are affected positively or negatively by the people we spend time with.

Think about it! Kids affect parents; parents affect kids. Spouses affect each other. The people we work with affect us negatively or positively, as do our friends, family, and neighbors.

There are times when we have little control over with whom we spend our time, especially at work. Seek someone at work who shares your vision for success.

Become a team member with successful people and help each other reach full potential. You cannot make it alone in your journey to success.

But be selective about those you choose as confidantes. You don't need someone to pull you down.

Let family members know about your new way of thinking, that speaking negatively about others or life in general has no place in your vocabulary. Tell them you love them, but let them know you're on a new path for success—for you, your family, and your friends.

You can have absolute control over your way of thinking!

*   *   *

Let's talk some more about friends. As mentioned earlier, Paw-Paw would say, "Go on with your life. You don't make friends; friends will happen!"

By being who you are, you'll find that true friends with good, solid values will surface, those who are positive thinkers like you!

You don't want people around you to say yes to everything you suggest. Trusted friends won't always slap you on the back and tout your virtues. They can, however, be very helpful as your harshest critics.

Paw-Paw always noted that those most interested in your personal growth and business life are those most interested in you—mentors who can point out your weaknesses and help you develop that area of your life to create strength.

We all need a coach. No one lives in a bubble.

We also need an open mind to seek out those with wisdom, like Paw-Paw. Often it takes *life experiences* and the loss of someone who gave tough love to look back and realize just how much you learned from that person. Unfortunately, most of us forget or aren't inclined to accept coaching from someone with only an LE.

*　　　　　*　　　　　*

Boxer and HBO sports commentator George Foreman first won the heavyweight championship of the world against an undefeated Joe Frazier in January of 1973. He had a saying: "There are always others trying to get to the same goal you are, only they decide to stop halfway down the road. And when they walk away, they leave the road paved for you."

With the power of positive thinking, he decided to become the heavyweight champion of the world for a second time at the age of 45. At that time, no one believed in George except himself and a couple of people around him. So he broke away from the naysayers—and made history by winning his second world heavyweight championship in November of 1994, two decades after his first. He was the oldest fighter to win it, and his record hasn't come close to being broken.

George learned a lot over the years, transitioning from "big strong man" in the early 1970s, to two-time world champion in the 1990s, to master salesman and motivational speaker today—from bully to teddy bear. George made the choice to hang around different people. He became a different person.

Acknowledge when a relationship sours. Go your separate way. No arguments, just realize that you have a difference in values and goals. Paw-Paw taught me that breaking away from friendships that drag you down is not bad, because a *true* friend exists to lift you up.

The First Teachers

By Amanda L. Guidry

The times Kerry spent on the front porch with Maw-Maw and Paw-Paw Daigle were just as educational as time spent at school. His school lessons of English, math, and science prepared him for the world. He learned to read, count money, and speak correctly. But those front porch lessons prepared him for life. He learned about people, about dignity and humility. He learned from his grandparents' wisdom.

Paw-Paw, whom Kerry describes as ruggedly handsome, was a bit short for a man at 5'11", owing to his French heritage. But he was strong, built like a bull, and quiet, never quick to jump to a conclusion.

Maw-Maw also was petite, probably never exceeding 100 pounds. With hazel eyes and a grinning countenance, her upbeat view of life inspired Kerry.

"Maw-Maw always had a smile and a laugh every day," reminisces Kerry, a similar smile playing at his mouth. "All anyone remembers about her is her laugh and smile. You could think of a thousand different features, but I remember that smile."

Maw-Maw would always remind him, "Kerry, when you see someone without a smile, give them yours. You could change their day or change their lives in that one moment. Never underestimate the power of a smile."

That porch…so many lessons.

Kerry with a smile (age 10)

Stinking Thinking

Anytime I suffered from a negative attitude, Maw-Maw and Paw-Paw would sit me down for a talk. They told me that the way in which I programmed myself in the morning would determine the outcome of my day. Because they couldn't read or write, they painted visual pictures for me instead.

Maw-Maw would tell Paw-Paw to take me out for a life lesson, to either a nursing home or a hospital. He made sure that I visited with others less fortunate than I: stroke victims, people in wheelchairs, young folks after an accident, anyone with physical disabilities.

Then we would walk back home in silence, to the porch where we sat.

73

"Do you really have a problem?" Paw-Paw would ask. "Or can we get rid of the stinking thinking?"

"We are not going to have any stinking thinking around here," said Maw-Maw Daigle. "No ifs, can'ts, won'ts, or buts."

Maw-Maw allowed no "stinking thinking" in my vocabulary. If I spoke in a negative tone, she quickly responded—often with a fly-swatter—and brought me to  my senses. She'd nip me on the side of the head or smack me on my rear and sternly admonish, "Kerry, we're not going to have any of that here."

In French, she set me straight: "Paw-Paw and I don't have an education. You know we can't read or write. We need you to be the strong one in our family, to teach us and watch over us. We will depend a lot on what you learn, and we need to start everything we do with the right attitude."

The words *can't, won't, if, but,* and *impossible* did not exist in our home. I always wanted my peers and friends to benefit from Maw-Maw's wisdom.

It seems that we need counselors to assist us with discouraging days when we forget the simple things such as a positive attitude. Maw-Maw taught me to remind myself that those negative words didn't exist unless we let them.

At eight years old, I didn't know any better. Funny how things work out. We become part of our environment. Although poor in the financial sense, our family was very wealthy in other ways.

Maw-Maw's teachings have since impacted my daughter, Angela, too. Adopted at age six, she was virtually homeless at the time. She couldn't read like most kids and didn't understand anything about having a family. By taking the words *can't, if, impossible,* and *won't* out of her vocabulary at an early age, we instilled positive self-esteem in Angela that brought her quickly up to speed. She became an honor roll student and graduated high school with awards and a 3.7 GPA. She is now attending college at LSU in Baton Rouge, Louisiana—an amazing change from the little girl we first met to the young woman she is today. Changing attitudes can have huge benefits.

Did that change happen because I had a college education that allowed me to teach her correctly? No. In fact, I am only a high school graduate. I simply believe that anyone can accomplish anything they set forth to do. Nothing is impossible. It's not magic—only the power of positive thoughts.

*   *   *

I remember another lesson hidden within the stories Paw-Paw told me about the old days.

Paw-Paw often talked about his parents' farm, and he knew a lot about planting crops. Every year, his family lived with nature, hurricanes, tornados, heat, frosts, dry spells, or too much rain.

He accepted what God brought and worked and toiled to the best of his ability with the rest of the family to deliver the best crop possible. Many times, the force of nature destroyed their work.

At no time did they ever quit. Paw-Paw gathered the family together, cleaned up the destruction, and moved forward, rebuilding the foundation for a new crop.

I would ask, "What kept you going, Paw-Paw?"

He answered simply and directly: "Sooner or later, if you don't quit, the good overrides the bad. Things happen to challenge you and see if you really want to succeed. Put the bad things behind you and think only of the good. Don't think of *if* things will work. Think that things *will* work."

Simple answer.

*   *   *

I learned early on that to move forward, we need to avoid stinking thinking in our lives.

When the *impossibles, ifs, won'ts,* and *can'ts* move into your vocabulary, you need to counteract them with the *cans, possibles,* and *wills.*

Sounds simple, but it's tough to train yourself in that direction if you've been trained to think negatively.

The best way to beat out the stinking thinking philosophies of life is to read books on personal development and positive thinking and to look at your environment. I'm glad you're getting some of Maw-Maw and Paw-Paw Daigle's wisdom from reading this short book. They're probably smiling right now watching you read this.

Who do you hang around with? Changing that alone can literally change your life.

One mentor of mine said, "You become what you read and who you hang around with. The only thing that changes your negativity toward life is to make changes in those areas."

Evaluate the people you associate with; get rid of those who drag you down. Start reading the books on personal development.

I constantly believe and state that a person who *doesn't* read is no better off than the person who *can't*.

Although it is not easy, you have to make simple decisions, simple changes that make the difference in your success financially, emotionally, and spiritually.

An important step is adding the word "believe" to your life vocabulary. Webster's defines *believe* as, "To have a firm conviction about something."

Why not believe in yourself? If you don't, who will?

To believe in yourself means to have the conviction that you *can* do certain things, you *will* do them, and everything *is* possible.

What if, 100 years ago, everyone believed that no one could build the airplane? What if no one believed we could have electric lights or a telephone?

Believing creates dreams. Dreams become fairy tales. Fairy tales turn into miracles. I know this is true. It's happened to me because Maw-Maw told me so.

If you want to know where you'll end up six years from now, write down the thoughts in your mind today. You can't see a thought, but you can follow it. Your body will follow your mind.

Your thoughts will become your habits.

Your habits will become part of your life.

Your family will follow in the footsteps of your habits.

Mark Twain once said, "Keep away from people who try to belittle your ambition. Small people always do that, but the really great make you feel that you, too, can become great."

Where are you headed? Do you believe?

Start dreaming again. Fairy tales will follow. Miracles can and will happen.

Just ask Maw-Maw.

Get Up and Get Out of Bed

One late afternoon after school, I felt particularly down on myself. I couldn't go to the prom; I was too embarrassed about my clothes, my poor circumstances.

Maw-Maw brought me out to the porch. For the first time, I saw her become livid. She reminded me that obstacles were no more than opportunities in disguise. She commanded me to be proud of my heritage. I remember she said that I may not understand until later, but that I'd better listen now.

Paw-Paw added his two cents from his chair: "Son, don't forget where you come from. That could be your biggest downfall. Remember who you are. Be humble and be proud of your background."

*　　　　　*　　　　　*

I can't remember who told me this little story, but I know you'll enjoy the message:

Tommy's mother called out to him at 6:30 in the morning, "Tommy, get up. It's time for school."

No answer.

She yelled at him again, in a much louder voice. "Tommy, get up! It's time for school!"

Again, no answer.

Aggravated, she went to his room and shook him, "Tommy, it's time for school."

Tommy answered, "Mom, I'm not going to school today. There are 1,000 kids at that school and every one of them hates me. I made up my mind—I'm not going!"

Tommy's mother replied quickly, in a stern voice, "You will go to school!"

Tommy tried again, "Mom, you don't understand! All the teachers hate me, too! I saw a group of them the other day pointing their fingers at me. I know they all hate me, Mom. I'm not going to school!"

Beyond frustrated, Tommy's mother cried out, "Get to school!"

"Mom," he replied, "I don't understand you at times. Why would you want to put me through so much embarrassment and torment?"

She answered quickly, "There are two reasons, Tommy. First, you are 45 years old. Second, you are the principal."

Most of us have felt like Tommy. It seems easier to skip out on the challenges that this game called life throws at us.

But life is about growing, not just surviving. Life is school, and we are its students.

To experience life at its fullest, we must be challenged every day. We must achieve accomplishments that live on as experiences that we can pass on to our children and others who seek our advice.

*　　　　　*　　　　　*

I have to go back to George Foreman, a mentor of mine through his books and his words. In his mid-forties, he was asked why he continued to train 5–7 hours a day, as no one had ever won a heavyweight championship at that age. He responded, "Because I think I am getting better and much wiser." As you know, George went on to become the oldest fighter in boxing history to win the heavyweight championship of the world.

When asked what his key to success was, George quoted the great British Prime Minister, Winston Churchill, "Never give up. Never, never give up."

Successful people have a history of turning defeat into victory and failure into success through a little more effort, a little more positive thinking, and a little more persistence than the average person.

Failure doesn't exist when you keep trying. You only get defeated within yourself.

Successful people get stronger through adversity, obstacles, and frustration. They keep punching even when knocked down. They get up and believe they will win despite any obstacles. They see obstacles as nothing more than opportunities in disguise, or, as. Maw-Maw called them, "tests" of the will to succeed.

No one can steal their dreams—not their friends, their families, envious associates, or competitors.

Every successful person's life carries a story of difficulty and challenge: no job, no money, business in bankruptcy, bills to be paid, family to support, abandoned friendships, and so much more. These challenges become fields of diamonds waiting for the harvest.

Sometimes life brings career changes that lead to advantages or opportunities for success in other arenas. Some people see these challenges as defeat without understanding that *how* we take on the challenge makes all the difference. For example, everything I own and am today came after a devastating bankruptcy.

*   *   *

Even after success, you will face challenges.

You may develop a tendency to become a teacher and forget to remain a student. That's when you might watch your success dissolve right in front of you.

To continue your success, you need to continue doing the things that brought you that success.

Zig Ziglar said it best: "Be more concerned about the success of others around you and success will ultimately be yours."

Consider this outline of Abraham Lincoln's road to success:

1831—Failure in business
1832—Defeated for Legislature
1833—Second failure in business
1836—Suffered nervous breakdown
1838—Defeated for Speaker
1840—Defeated for Elector
1843—Defeated for Congress
1848—Defeated for Congress, again
1855—Defeated for Senate
1856—Defeated for Vice-President
1858—Defeated for Senate, again
1860—*Elected President of the United States!*

What about you? As Paw-Paw Daigle would ask me, "What's your next move?"

Kerry in the U.S. Army National Guard, 1970

Attitude Is the Key to Your Success

Did you know that you decide whether you have a good day or a bad day? And you determine whether you are going to be successful or not. It's your decision!

I remember speaking to a group of college students in April of 1997 at St. Joseph's University in Philadelphia, where I was invited to give an inspirational talk. My host was Richard George, a professor of marketing at the university and the author of the bestselling book *Success Leaves Clues*. I was quite honored, because Richard is regarded by his peers as an outstanding personal development coach and is a trainer to many Fortune 500 companies.

That day, as I watched these young students, I saw the same things I see in groups of would-be entrepreneurs. Some came into the seminar and sat up front with notepads and eyes gleaming. Others walked in late, carrying drinks and cell phones, slouching in their chairs at the back of the room, their eyes very distant. Some sought advice and looked for mentorship, while others just wondered why they were there and had absolutely no clue!

That leads me to a small word that can, literally, alter your life: attitude!

Have you ever noticed the people who go through life as walking zombies? What I mean by that is they were born in the 1970s, died in the 1990s, but will be buried in this century. Their attitudes were so terrible that somewhere between the '70s and this new millennium they lost their zeal for enjoying life. Their attitude shows! They are what I call the "walking dead."

These walking dead wake up with a frown and complaint, crawl to the bathroom to prepare for the day, leave home in a hurry, slamming the door and kicking the cat while yelling at their spouse and kids, and drive off with their minds on hating what they do! Have you ever met that person? Usually, there is only one in your community. He or she just moves around a lot. When asked by coworkers, "What's going on?" these people generally reply, "Aw, nothin'. Just work!"

Now here's the real weirdo in some eyes: She gets up, kisses her husband and kids good morning, walks to the bathroom, and looks in the mirror with a big smile—you can see all of her teeth. She leaves home, telling everyone to have a good day and thanking God that she woke up again to a glorious morning. She has another day and yet another challenge. Someone asks this person how she's doing, and she answers immediately with enthusiasm and a big smile, "Great! And you?"

It's called *attitude*!

It is your attitude toward life that will determine life's attitude toward you. You must mentally become the person you want to be. You and only you can make that choice.

*   *   *

Melvin Turner, a business associate of mine from Louisville, Kentucky, is a university professor who gives public speaking sessions on attitude. He is known for being one of many to have assisted and encouraged Les Brown, the famous motivational speaker and well-known author of several books including *Live Your Dreams*. (Les Brown commands a fee in the vicinity of $30,000 or more for a speaking session of about an hour and a half.)

Melvin is a perfect example of a happy individual who looks forward to life's challenges every day. He uses the word "attitude" as an acronym for the inspirational phrases below (his phrases are underlined, followed by my notes):

Activate your potentials.

I define that as using your God-given skills. Everyone has a love or skill. It's what you do with that skill that counts.

Turn all negatives into positives.

My read on this is that problems are nothing more than hidden opportunities to test you. Take them on!

Try with all your might and success will follow.

In other words, be focused and never give up! Don't let anyone steal your dreams!

Imagination is the key to self-development.

Dream and dream big! If you can envision what you want, it can happen to you.

Tune into the positive side of life.

That means you may have to give up some negative friends. Why would you want to be around people who pull you down? Find a successful mentor and follow in those footsteps.

Unique is the individual you are.

You are special! We all have special gifts. What you do with them is what is important.

Develop yourself now.

I believe everyone should invest 3–5 percent of their gross monthly income in themselves by purchasing personal development material such as motivational tapes and self-help books so they can become better people. Read positive books, listen to recordings of positive people, and follow their teachings. Be a better you and keep working on it. Make your automobile a rolling university on tape.

Express and enjoy life.

Be happy you woke up this morning. As Paw-Paw Daigle used to say, "Some people didn't wake up this morning."

*   *   *

Here are my personal ten principles to follow for success. I wrote these down over two decades ago after some interesting challenges in my life, and I never looked back at my misfortunes.

1. Respond to situations. Don't react!
2. Be a student, and find successful people with positive attitudes to become your mentors.
3. Don't burn bridges. You might have to cross them someday.
4. When you are wrong and make mistakes, accept the facts and then learn from them. Move forward! Make that a chapter in your book of life.
5. Always have a sense of urgency and a fear of loss.
6. Write down your goals every week. Complete them and check them off. Be productive in your new life.

7. Insist on success. Don't let anyone steal your dreams!

8. People don't care how much you know; they want to know how much you care. Treat people with dignity, and they will treat you the same.

9. Swallow your ego. Be confident but not egotistical. Remember to always be a student, not just a teacher.

10. When life knocks you down, get up! Don't ever let anyone knock you out. Keep punching!

Get Motivated: Dream Big

When I first wanted to get involved with professional boxing, my friends shot down my dream. They told me that I would fail because I didn't have a college degree or the financial backing necessary to succeed. They reminded me that I had no connections because of my family background.

I began to doubt myself, and I poured my heart out to Maw-Maw.

She sat me down early one morning over coffee and suggested I stop hanging around negative, doubting people. She said I should find my friends from good books.

She helped me use my background to motivate me to work harder.

Maw-Maw told me, "You have the power to dream and dream big. You can do things you never thought you could do, if you believe in your dream. There are no limits to your accomplishments except the limits you set in your own mind."

*   *   *

A young lady recently asked me at a function where I was a keynote speaker, "How do I get motivated and stay motivated?" That question comes up all the time.

The answer may seem simple, though the journey itself will have its ups and downs.

First, we must remember that until we make the positive changes, the task will feel difficult. Once we make them, great things begin to happen. It all starts with attitude and action.

Step one is to invest in yourself by purchasing audio programs and books on motivation and personal development. As mentioned previously, make your automobile a rolling university by listening to daily inspirational messages.

Seek out one or two points from each of those resources that may assist you in your goals to become a better, more positive person. Don't worry about absorbing everything over-night.

Turn off sensationalist shock-jocks and tune in to interviews with top authors and experts in the fields of personal growth, inspiration, motivation, and positive thinking. These masters will lead you to understand what works best for you.

If you constantly feed yourself positive thoughts, you will plant them in your mind where they'll begin to grow and become part of who you are.

You can feed your mind positive thoughts or negative ones. You have complete control over that decision. It is your choice and yours alone.

What happens with your day and how you respond to situations determines its outcome.

Use simple philosophy.

Respond to situations, don't react. Don't get caught up in an emotional or negative answer. Paw-Paw said it's always best to sleep on an answer to a tough question or decision before answering with an emotion that may haunt you for the rest of your life.

As the industrialist Andrew Carnegie wrote, "The man who acquires the ability to take full possession of his own mind may take possession of anything else to which he is justly entitled."

Next, set goals for yourself on paper. Write them down, starting with long-term goals and then breaking them into years, months, weeks, days, and parts of days.

Be specific. Devise a plan. And don't overwhelm yourself. I believe in *whelming*, not *overwhelming*.

Set realistic goals that you know you can reach even though you also realize that you'll have to put out effort to reach them. Every home is built one brick at a time. We never start with the roof.

You have to make plans and goals before starting, and it starts one day at a time. Be patient and fair to yourself.

Completing small goals regularly brings you to your larger goal.

Carry a day planner with you everywhere. List your daily accomplishments. Keep a record of what you achieve.

To develop a positive new lifestyle, talk to yourself in a positive voice. When you think negative thoughts, tell yourself to cancel those negative thoughts. Eventually, you'll train yourself to ban those from your mind.

Never think you don't have the talent or ability to succeed. Neither education nor background should be a factor. You can always acquire education, formally or on your own, depending on your goals. The only thing that counts is your attitude toward yourself.

Every individual has a gift or talent and needs to utilize that gift to its fullest potential.

But if you don't believe in yourself, how can someone else believe in you?

There may be times when people tell you that you don't have skills or talents. You may need to dig deep in your soul and heart to find courage. You may need to use every bit of intestinal fortitude to say, "Yes, I can. Yes, I will do the things necessary for success."

It's about taking action and changing things you're unhappy with.

Continue to educate yourself with books and tapes. Motivational speaker Jim Rohn says it best: "Educate then motivate." Listen to the tapes, read the books, get an attitude adjustment, then turn on your enthusiasm. Smile regularly and watch your personality become contagious.

Last but not least, be responsible for yourself. Make good choices.

Some people want to change the world, and that's okay, but let's be realistic. Although you may not change the entire world, you can change your personal world by making good choices about what you read, what you watch, what you listen to, you associate with, and what thoughts you accept or reject.

Don't get caught up in doing negative things others may do to be part of a crowd. Cultivate integrity and choose to be different.

Remember, if you want to fly with the eagles, wading in a pool of quacking ducks is a waste of your time.

*　　　　*　　　　*

Because Maw-Maw and Paw-Paw instilled in me that you have to dream big, in my early twenties I became involved in my dream of promoting professional boxing and managing professional fighters. I started doing business with national and international television executives throughout the world with only a high school education.

Did my lack of a formal education stop me? Did my background stop me?

If anything, my background motivated me to move forward. Maw-Maw and Paw-Paw instilled in me the power of the dream.

Embrace Success

I will forever cherish the lessons I learned on the front porch. I can still see Maw-Maw and Paw-Paw sitting in their chairs, watching the cars go by and dispensing profound wisdom.

My path was shaped by their words. I know they watch me from above. They still talk to me every day. In the face of any obstacle, they always knew what to say.

When it comes to almost every aspect of life, Paw-Paw expressed it best: "The best way to get on your feet is to get off your butt." I used to laugh when he would say that. Even today it brings a big smile. Regardless, he was right. Thanks, Paw-Paw.

*   *   *

As I travel the globe, the same question frequently recurs: "What does it take to be successful?"

Too often we hear these attributions:

- "He was lucky."
- "She fell into it."
- "Everything she touches turns to gold."
- "Money makes money."
- "You have to have money to become successful."

Despite a measure of truth, these are not completely accurate. It depends largely on interpretation.

Some people use those same statements as excuses for their non-success. It's easier to blame circumstances than to admit that you don't want to pay a price for success.

But in that case, the underlying message rings clear: "If I have to put sweat equity into play, then I prefer to be mediocre."

Let's understand success. Webster's dictionary defines it as "a favorable course or the termination of anything attempted; the gaining of position, fame, wealth, etc.; achievement."

Consider this part of the definition: "the termination of anything attempted." Just because you've attempted to do something and have stopped doesn't mean you've been un-successful. It means you've quit!

You may need to attempt something several times before you achieve any success with it.

Success means different things to different people. Some people attach the word "success" to financial security, a successful career, power, or political positioning. Others attribute success to the ability to have a job, a nicer home, a newer car.

I like Wynn Davis's description in his book *The Best of Success*: "Success means doing the best we can with what we have. Success is in the doing, not the getting, in the trying, not the triumph. Success is a personal standard reaching for the highest that is in us becoming all that we can be. If we do our best, we have been successful."

*   *   *

To achieve any level of success, we must have a plan.

There are no shortcuts.

It is about sweat equity. Sweat equity means you have to go to work.

Turn off the television.

Take care of yourself physically.

Think positively.

Rid yourself of negative people.

Make tough choices.

Why is the television called the boob-tube? What does that mean? Figure it out! You ask, "I must take care of myself physically, give up cigarettes, give up my beer every evening, and start exercising? You want me to get rid of negative friends and relatives?"

Yes, success comes with a price tag. It means unloading the stinking thinking that surrounds you.

What I learned along the way to success is that successful people have one thing in common. They believe every goal will be achieved, under any and all circumstances, despite any and all obstacles, no matter how long it takes.

Anyone can cry and whine about how difficult it is to overcome obstacles. What a surprise! Everyone has obstacles to overcome and endures trials and tribulations before achieving success. The successful don't accept roadblocks or mediocrity.

A successful disposition or attitude can be seen in a person's eyes. Have you ever looked into someone's eyes and seen nothing there?

They seem void of life in general, while others have that sparkle.

The bright-eyed people don't cry or complain. They find solutions and turn problems into opportunities. They enthuse you with their attitudes.

Life isn't fair. So what? You must tackle unfair events with integrity, forcefulness, and the intestinal fortitude to overcome your problem.

The "worst" thing for my friends and family to do is to come to me complaining about their problems. They know that after listening, I'll immediately ask, "What are you going to do about this problem today?" I'll then formulate a plan with them to overcome the problem and help them write out a goal sheet.

Then we'll work on instilling the motivation and inspiration needed to move forward—that's the part where most people fall short. That is why most people live in mediocrity. They won't step forward to attempt to achieve their goals. They fail before they even start.

*   *   *

I know something about you: you are a human being. Humans are smart creatures. Humans are extremely wise. Humans know how to look out after themselves. They have the ability to work hard.

We are all made of the same material. Some of us decide to do better and adopt a different attitude.

Believe in yourself. Let your subconscious mind agree with your beliefs.

Negative thinking is no different from alcoholism or drug use. You've got to quit that behavior! Human beings have that ability. Why would you choose any other behavior?

On your way to success, there are no failures. There are only roadblocks and obstacles to test the strength of your mind. Failures step you toward success. Small failures lead to small successes. Small successes lead to larger ones.

When something doesn't work, create a new starting point and go for it again.

Life may trip us up from time to time. It takes more tries for some than for others. Who cares? Who cares if it takes longer, as long as you get there? It all starts with your decision to be successful.

Colonel Harland Sanders of Kentucky Fried Chicken fame finally achieved financial success in his mid-sixties. Formulated in 1939, his fried chicken recipe was rejected by hundreds of potential investors for many years. His first franchise opened in 1952 in Salt Lake City, Utah, 13 years after he began his quest.

Col. Sanders said, "I made a resolve then that I was going to amount to something if I could. And no hours, nor amount of labor, nor amount of money, would deter me from giving the best that there was in me. And I have done that ever since, and I win by it. I know."

No words better said.

Kind of reminds me of Paw-Paw Daigle.

Get Out of Your Comfort Zone

Maw-Maw and Paw-Paw Daigle constantly urged me to buy books.

"Read, read, read," they would say, even though they couldn't read a word. For 15–30 minutes every day, I sat on the porch—sometimes with them, sometimes alone—often translating what I read into French. We had no television. Reading became my main source of entertainment.

Maw-Maw said to me, "Paw-Paw and I can neither read nor write, but you can. Son, remember this: the person who doesn't read books is no better off than the person who can't read. Read the right books, the ones that will educate you and move your life forward."

*   *   *

Henry Emerson Fosdick, a master preacher and author of 47 books, wrote: "Have the daring to accept yourself as a bundle of possibilities and undertake the game of making the most of your best."

Arnold Glasow, the American humorist, wrote: "Cultivate the qualities in yourself what you admire the most in others."

Another quote I remember is: "Today a reader, tomorrow a leader."

Where does this lesson take you?

A consistent personal development program will achieve the things mentioned in these quotes. Making the most of your best comes from constantly having positive thoughts. Cultivating qualities in yourself from what you admire the most in others happens when you find true and inspiring mentors.

We all know what reading will do. We've heard the old axiom "knowledge is power."

True, in a sense, although knowledge on ice doesn't help you in any way. Knowledge itself is not power. *Applied* knowledge is power. A 23-year-old entrepreneur, Travis Broussard, taught me this years ago.

You have to perform. You must be productive, not active, and understand the difference between productivity and activity.

You need to grow personally. To grow and develop is very stimulating and exciting. With personal growth, we step out of our comfort zone and do what others won't do.

Only 5 percent of Americans enjoy financial success and earn a six-figure income; 95 percent earn substantially less. Do you believe the 5 percent are different from the 95 percent?

Of course they are. Everything they do is different. They are different.

The thrill of becoming successful and leading an exciting life has everything to do with stretching out beyond what you think is possible and constantly attempting to do better.

You must want to become the person you were not yesterday. A positive attitude will give you a completely different perspective on life, an almost superhuman power that allows you to handle all obstacles and view them only as challenges that test you. The daily problems don't appear so bad when you constantly work on personal self-development.

Or you can have the complete opposite—hang around negative people long enough, and, sure enough, you will become negative.

You decide.

You must continue to develop your leadership and personal development skills for success to happen. Great things are not accomplished by impulse but by a series of small things done well on a consistent basis.

My wife Mickey and I developed a hugely successful direct-sales home-based business that pays a very handsome income residually, which would have allowed me to retire if I chose to at the age of 42. That business was built on consistent daily efforts, sometimes only 2–3 hours a day, but consistently every day.

If you develop yourself through reading and listening to self-empowerment tapes, you will enter an entirely different playing field.

The person in business who chooses to get comfortable, who goes through the motions of work every day without enthusiasm, eventually settles for mediocrity. To step away from mediocrity, we must perform at a high standard and set goals that will enhance our career with a continuous program of self-improvement and personal development.

Read the books.

Listen to the tapes.

Changing your current habits into positive thinking will challenge you. You may have to give up associates and friends who drag you down. I don't want to sound redundant, but I do want to deliver this message deep into your subconscious mind.

Remember this: It does not matter how you feel in the short term. You must work at changing your frame of mind over a longer period of time and constantly exercise your thoughts as you would a muscle in physical exercise.

After 20, 30, or 40 years of negative thinking, four to five years of positive personal development is not long to make dramatic changes in your life physically, mentally, spiritually, and financially.

I compare a program of self-improvement to managing a professional prizefighter. You wouldn't let a recently-turned-professional fight in his pro debut against a world champion, would you?

Of course not!

He (or even she, nowadays) would start his career training exceptionally hard. The first fight would be four rounds. He'd then fight a series of four-round fights before moving into six-round fights, then eight rounds, and eventually into ten-round main event fights. Throughout, the fighter would learn and learn, train and train. Only then could he commit to a championship challenge for 12 rounds.

We must all take "baby steps" first.

Vince Lombardi noted that the outcomes of most football games are decided in "feet and inches." And we've all heard the old Chinese saying, "The journey of a thousand miles begins with a single step."

How far have you walked today in your quest for success?

Look forward, never backward.

Approach your life with a vision. Follow it without letting anyone put blinders over your eyes.

Work at your goals regularly, inch by inch, step by step, day by day. If you do, I guarantee that you will find much more success in your life.

If anyone accuses you of being brainwashed, respond with these words: "You know, you're right! I am being brainwashed with positive thoughts. I made that choice after being brainwashed with negative ones for too long. Those days are history. I am moving forward. Will you join me? If not, step aside!"

*   *   *

Maw-Maw and Paw-Paw: thank you for teaching me in those early years that anyone can do or be whatever they want to be. Success is about making a decision. Choices are plentiful. I know you are still watching me because you promised you would. I hear your voices every day. Keep teaching me and I promise to give these same gifts to others to honor your requests that I do so.

I'll always keep punching!

Epilogue

I sincerely hope that over these pages of wisdom from Maw-Maw and Paw-Paw Daigle, along with lessons from some of my other mentors, I've given you something to take away and utilize for your own business and personal success. To really benefit from this book, you need to be willing to make changes in your thought processes; in the way you look at your work, career, and classes (if you're still in school); and most importantly, in your life.

Your job now is to teach others. There are a number of ways you can use this book as a means of sharing stories. If you're giving the book to someone, be certain to write a personal note to the recipient. Together, they become a gift that is remembered for a lifetime.

The principles discussed in *Dreams, Fairy Tales, and Miracles* are simple and easily applied to everyday life. Maw-Maw and Paw-Paw always believed in the power of giving, feeling that giving would enhance both life and career and bring tenfold spiritual and emotional rewards, which would instantly bring material rewards as well. It's almost magical.

If you believe in your dreams and apply them to your work, you will become a star in your own career. You can be a star salesperson, a star accountant, a star home-based business owner, a star athlete, a star performer in any field you choose.

By implanting gratitude in your thoughts every day and appreciating what you *do* have instead of what you *don't* have, you will eventually live a fairy tale life. Maw-Maw told me when you reach that stage of gratitude, miracles start happening. I know it's true, as I am a miracle and so are you. We are all miracles.

Be sure to thank those people who've made an impact in your life. Send out hand-written thank-you cards, even to people you haven't spoken to for years. You will be surprised at how good you'll feel and at the magic that will come from such a simple gesture.

I'm hoping you're spreading Maw-Maw and Paw-Paw's words of wisdom to those you care about within your family, friends, and those you work with. I hope Maw-Maw and Paw-Paw have touched you as they touched me. As Maw-Maw always said, "If you see someone without a smile...give them yours."

I'll tell them you said hello.

Kerry with boxing great George Foreman

Kerry with "The Golden Boy" Oscar De La Hoya

Kerry with trainer Angelo Dundee